A Model for Christian Youth Work

Nigel Pimlott

Deputy Chief Executive Officer, Frontier Youth Trust

GROVE BOOKS LIMITED

RIDLEY HALL RD CAMBRIDGE CB3 9HU

Contents

Acknowledgment
With special thanks to The Institute for Children, Youth and Mission, Oasis College and
Staffordshire University for funding the original work informing this booklet.

First Impression June 2015
ISSN 1748–3492
ISBN 978 1 85174 941 6

Introduction

This is a booklet written to help those who wish to undertake work with young people. It is not a 'how to' booklet in the sense of providing resources for weekly sessions with young people. However, it is a 'how to' booklet that invites youth workers to take a step back from the day-to-day challenges and opportunities of Christian youth work. It is an invitation to pause, reflect and appraise what exactly it is that the youth work they have undertaken is trying to achieve.

In my work with Frontier Youth Trust (FYT), I have had the fantastic privilege of meeting thousands of people who work with young people. These workers come from all sorts of backgrounds and denominations, working in a wide variety of churches and projects. Some workers are employed, some volunteers; some have qualifications, many do not. Often I meet people with lots of experience, and sometimes meet those just starting out in their service of young people. What I have noticed is that it is not always clear what people are trying to achieve in their work and even less tangible how they are going to go about it.

The danger of not knowing what we are trying to achieve is that we drift from this to that

The danger of not knowing what we are trying to achieve is that we just drift from this to that, wandering around from here to there, a bit like Moses in the desert. Other biblical characters had a very clear sense of purpose.

Noah knew what he was about and Joseph, Nehemiah and Ruth had a clear quest and goal.[1] John the Baptist was very precise about what he needed to accomplish as he prepared the way for Jesus, and the apostle Paul would not let anything distract him from his mission. Those very clever ancient Greeks came up with a word to describe this type of purpose: that aim, ultimate intention or end point that the above characters were so focused on. They called it the *telos*.

I have noticed that modern-day youth workers and ministers are not always clear about their *telos*. Sometimes the employed youth worker, board of trustees and/or church minister has a clear sense of what the *telos* is. However, my research has identified that the focus of any *telos* often becomes diminished amongst those part-time and volunteer workers involved in a project or church. In other words, even where senior leaders know what they are trying to do, others appear less certain.

My hope is that by using the model to identify the key aspects of your youth work, everybody involved in serving young people will have a clearer sense of what they are about and what it is they are trying to do. This might not happen overnight, so my encouragement is to read the following pages, think about how they relate to your context and decide if how you currently operate might need a bit of adjustment so your focus and intentions are clear for all to see.

The Case for Ensuring Clarity

The very first Grove Youth booklet (Y1) explored how we might best be *Responding to Challenging Behaviour*.[2] Since that booklet was written I and my FYT colleagues have delivered well over 100 training sessions on the subject. During the training I usually ask participants what it is they are trying to achieve in their work with young people. I do this in order to highlight how having a clear intention helps embed a sense of collective purpose for the work and provides clear boundaries within which it can exist, whilst offering a framework out of which our message of hope and love to young people can emerge. Once these things are in place, I observe, it becomes easier to respond with precision and consistency to challenging behaviour issues. I am sad to report that in many training sessions people have not known what it is they are trying to achieve and, consequently, responding to challenging behaviours becomes all the more difficult as there is not a shared and collective *telos* which everybody is working towards.

This lack of clarity, in worst case scenarios, actually causes work to be shut down. I worked with a church recently that was attracting large numbers of young people to a club night. The young people became unruly and chaos ensued. Church leaders lost confidence in the lead worker and the project, and they closed down the work. When I chatted to them about the project, it was clear that, despite its numerical successes, no one knew what the project was ultimately aiming for.

I have also encountered uncertainty because of, for example:

- Churches and projects always wondering what the next step is, but never quite nailing anything down;

- People and pieces of work ending up compromised because the terms and conditions of a funding pot or work contract dictate what they do, not their Spirit-inspired *telos*;

- Theological and trendy ecclesiological whims diverting individuals and groups away from their primary callings;

- Fear, calamity and despair as people become lost in a spiritual desert where no one is excited or has a sense of vision, and everybody is downtrodden and despondent;

- Everybody floundering in a whirlpool of over-excitement, charisma, unaccountable prophetic euphoria and/or ecstatic worship pictures that are always talking up what might happen but, again, never really establishing what this might be.

These scenarios are all too common and, in my experience, the consequences of this 'not knowing' are:

- A lack of vision, people, money, resources and energy to do the youth work;

- A propensity to give up when things get tough;

- High staff and volunteer turnover;

- Misunderstandings over theology, practical considerations, or relationships with stakeholders;

- Poor community relationships; and

- Poor recruitment decisions. In my work with FYT, my colleagues and I come across far too many situations where the recruitment process has not gone to plan. Typically, we discover scenarios where the leadership of the church think the youth work job is about one thing, the church leader or minister think something slightly different, the church congregation think it is about something different still, and the worker believes it is what they interpret it to be. The results can lead to tensions, misunderstandings and sometimes very big fall outs—all because of a lack of clarity about what the *telos* is.

Of course, some people are very content just plodding through life, trying a bit of this and a piece of that, dabbling here, ministering there. There is a lovely section in Lewis Carroll's 1865 novel, *Alice's Adventures in Wonderland*, that beautifully highlights how this approach undermines our direction and *telos*. It goes like this:

Alice: 'Would you tell me, please, which way I ought to go from here?'
Cheshire Cat: 'That depends a good deal on where you want to get to.'
Alice: 'I don't much care where.'
Cheshire Cat: 'Then it doesn't matter which way you go.'

Our personalities and individual characteristics often determine our approach to things. Irrespective of this, I remain convinced that God is a god who is on a mission and he invites us to be part of that; I believe God does care which way we go. If this is the case then we must discern what God's mission is at any one point in time and then join in with it—what theologians call the *missio Dei*. This necessitates having a clear strategy and set of plans and aims, born out of prayer, reflection and revelation.

For Reflection

If you wanted to discover if everyone in your context knew what you were trying to do, you could—as a piece of reflective research—ask each individual connected with your work (staff, volunteers, partners, young people, governors, leaders etc) for three words or phrases that they would use to describe what you are aiming to achieve. You could see if people come up with similar words or ideas. If they do, you can probably put this booklet down and go and do something else. If they do not, then I would encourage you to read on…

Why Use a Model?

I often observe that Christian youth workers are passionate, creative and committed people who make sacrifices to serve the young people they work with and for. Some are even prepared to become foolish in order to serve the God they love (1 Cor 4.10). However, I am convinced that passion, creativity, commitment, sacrifice and a willingness to be foolish are not in themselves sufficient if these qualities are not channelled in a purposeful way. We need to ensure we align and intentionally shape our actions so they fully reflect our passions, values, vision and aspirations. A model helps with this.

Those who have no experience of, or do not do, youth work often do not 'get it.' A model not only helps position work effectively; it also enables others to better understand what youth workers are doing and why. This helps increase understanding, ownership of the work, support for it and communication about it. A model simplifies the complexity of what Christian youth work is and all that it involves and turns its multifaceted nature into a powerful, impacting and easy to understand process.

A model offers something to build upon and a way of moving toward a goal. I love watching TV design, renovation and building programmes. People do some amazing things, but their projects often go wrong or way over budget if they do not have a plan or an end goal in sight. Maybe my love of these programmes is why my model is orientated around a house (details coming up).

A model enables us to track the progress we are making

A model also enables us to track the progress we are making. In my model this can be done against each element of the model. Some people prefer diagrams and pictures to words on a page. My model is a visual one that will appeal to such people, enabling a visual representation of what is happening to be conveyed to everybody involved. This can further help improve communication and understanding.

I do not believe a model should be restrictive and constraining, but more what I would call *intentionally guiding and shaping* what might be: it should be a process and a tool to help us do what we do more easily and effectively. If a model does not do this, then I would not use it. All models endeavour to help us work more smartly. They seek to help us move from one place to a better place, answering questions, provoking responses and prompting solutions as we go. My PhD studies investigated and set about answering a series of questions to try and develop a model that would be of help to youth workers and ministers.

I wanted to know:

- The place, position and characteristics of faith in any work undertaken. In other words, I wanted to see where God was in the work so that I could establish *why* people do Christian-motivated youth work.

- The shape of what the youth work was—defining its values in order to determine *how* such work is undertaken.

- What the intentions of the youth work undertaken were—identifying specific theories and practices of the work; understanding *what* work is actually undertaken.

As my research developed I was able to develop a model that helped answer these questions and put in place a process others could follow and adapt.

My Model

As mentioned, my model is based upon the image or metaphor of a house or building. In it, I would like to suggest that our youth work or ministry should have a firm foundation, then a series of metaphorical floors determining what our work should look like and be made up of (I have called these the *grounding*, *shape*, *intentions* and *outcomes*), and then a roof, representing what we are aiming for—that *telos* previously described. If we looked at a side view of the building incorporating these ideas, it would look like this:

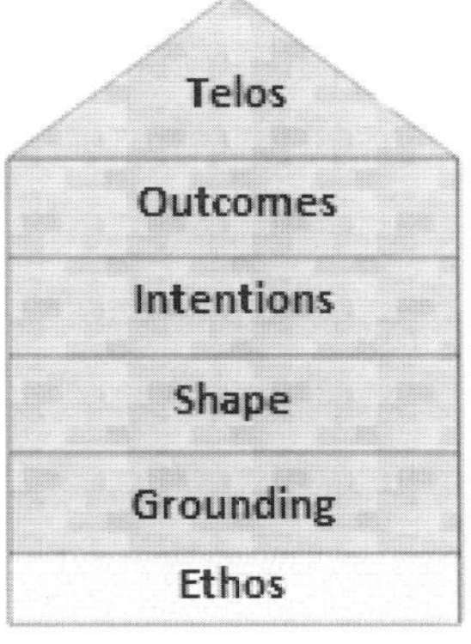

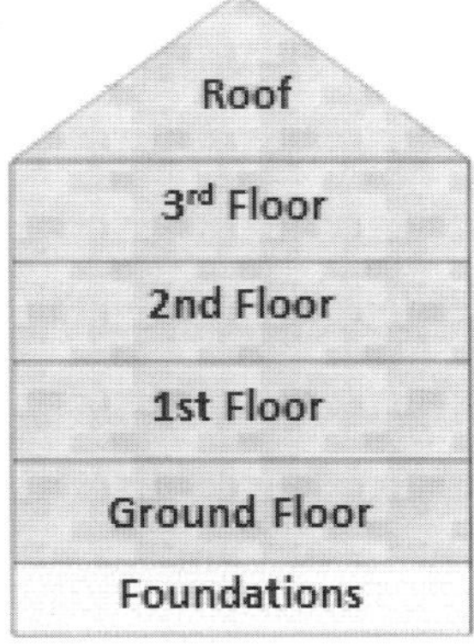

I have called the *foundations* the ethos—that driving set of beliefs, character and fundamentals of what we are about. Next comes the *grounding*—the big idea, belief, theory or sense of calling that God has laid upon us: the ground floor through which everything has to go to progress up the building. This is followed by the *first floor*—the shape the work will take and the values and philosophy underpinning it. Then there is the *second floor*—the intentions, actions and methods that will be used in delivering the work. This is what educationalists might call the pedagogy: those principles, approaches and nature of education that we use to do the work. The last floor represents the *outcomes* that will be achieved—the transformation and difference our work and ministry will make. Finally, as discussed, there is the *telos*, representing the roof and highest point of the building—the ultimate purpose or aim of what we are seeking to do.

To begin the process of using the model, I have used the various spaces in the building to trigger a series of questions that begin to unpack the model further:

For Reflection

You may wish to spend some time (either on your own or with your youth work team) thinking about these questions before reading on. As the sections proceed, you will be asked to think a little more deeply about each metaphorical part of the building.

The Ultimate Purpose or Aim

In order to enable this model to work most effectively, we need to think about our *telos* first. We need to think about what it is we are trying to achieve and what that might look like in its most successful form. In the model, the *telos* is represented by the roof of the building.

In a letter to the Italian historian and poet, Benedetto Varchi, the great artist and sculptor Michelangelo said, 'I saw the angel in the marble and carved until I set him free.' In other words, from a block of stone or marble, Michelangelo saw what it was he wanted to create and he then began the process of realizing what he saw, setting free the vision that was within. I think this is what I mean by the *telos*. What is it that we see in our work with young people and what is it that we need to set free in order for that to become everything we hope and dream? If you like, it is the same sentiment found in the book of Hebrews when the author says 'Faith is being sure of what we hope for and certain of what we do not see' (Heb 11.1). Once we have this hope, belief and certainty of mind, I believe we can then start building and working towards realizing the dream.

We might witness our *telos* in something God is calling us to, a vision, a promise, a quest or prophetic belief that builds the kingdom of God. Whilst, to continue to draw on the Letter to the Hebrews, we might not actually have full evidence and see what it actually is in full detail, we know it to be true in our minds that God has spoken, that our purpose is clear and our spiritual imperative is understood. We recognize it in our bones, deep in our bowels (as the Bible often terms it) to be our *telos* because it—whatever *it* is—releases energy within and beyond.

For example, I met a youth worker recently who was very clear that his *telos* was to work so that young people:

> ...reach unity in the faith and in the knowledge of the Son of God and become mature, attaining to the whole measure of the fullness of Christ.

His ultimate aim was based on this verse from Eph 4.13. His youth ministry was designed to realize this aspiration.

My *telos* and model of mission over the last twenty years have been to make people think about themselves, the world they live in and God, so that: they experience a bit of God; are motivated to seek *shalom*; and exist to build a better world.[3] More recently, I have refined this to encompass ideas about helping people flourish and build the common good. This is my quest and, I believe, calling.

For Reflection

If you do not know what your *telos* is, then my encouragement is to spend some time thinking about what it might be. You may wish to enlist the help of others to help you on this journey of discovery. If you do know what it is, or as soon as you do, then I would further encourage you to put in place people and processes that help realize it: support, prayer, resources, confidants, critical friends, and fellow pilgrims.

At some point the *telos* will need to be communicated to a wider audience. It may be that the *telos* has been developed as part of a group, church or community. I think this a good thing and I would not wish to communicate that having a *telos* is just an individualistic matter—a collective *telos* is a positive attribute. Young people, colleagues and other stakeholders may have shaped the *telos* and others may be aware of what it is. However, it is worth reiterating—in simple concise terms—what it is you are about to as many people as possible. This helps set the scene for determining why we do what we do.

Case Study

Worth Unlimited is an organization working to address the needs of marginalized and excluded young people throughout the UK. They have a strapline that says they are about 'Building hope, unlocking potential and realizing worth in young people.' However, their strapline is more than a description of what they do: it is a summary of their ultimate purpose and it keeps them focused on what they do, who they do it with and how they go about doing it.

Why Do We Do what We Do?

5

I met a vicar recently who was grappling with new ideas about church and ways of doing it. She had spent many decades doing church the same way and really enjoyed her traditional approach. She saw no need to do anything differently and had no motivation to do so. A few days later, I also talked to a youth work colleague. Every few years he feels the need to do something different. He is not motivated by doing the same thing week in, week out.

These two conversations illustrate that people are different. They are wired differently, have different approaches to life and ministry and have different motivations. These different motivations might be related to serving young people, building the church, changing the world, regenerating a community or, as I have described for me, promoting the common good. They might also relate to an individual sense of calling, guilt, the pursuit of self-actualization or a need to be affirmed or valued. Whatever the motivation to do something is, I believe it is always good to ask ourselves why we do what we do.

In my experience, this question is not asked often enough in church and Christian settings. I am sure we do many things simply because we are Christians and that is what Christians do (or should do), or because we want to 'love God,' 'love our neighbour' or seek *shalom*. However, I consider that we need to delve deeper than this when thinking about why we undertake youth work and ministry. In my model, I call this sense of knowing by another Greek term, the *ethos*.

What ethos makes us do what we do? What are the foundations upon which we can build the work we do? The simplistic (and no doubt valid) answer is that *Jesus* is the foundation and cornerstone of our ministry (Eph 2.20). My dilemma in saying this is that it is too easy to fall into the trap of fitting Jesus into our own worldview and agenda—we end up making Jesus fit our image. Which Jesus is your foundation: healer; saviour; politician; lover; radical subversive; guru; solver of problems; meeter of needs; granter of wishes; and/or? The list could go on and on.

My encouragement is to go deeper than rattled-off over-simplistic interpretations of Bible verses that we are prone to trotting out now and again. When talking about the ethos of our work, my encouragement is to really hone in on the thing or things that motivate us to do what we do. For example, it might be that our faith compels us to try and make our community better and serving young people enables this. We might want to speak to those people and powers that often denigrate and marginalize young people by speaking up for them. We might have deep convictions that slavery, abuse, homelessness, poverty, injustice and/or youth unemployment are terrible slurs on humanity and be motivated to work with young people so that they do not become victims of these matters. We might have a passion for worship and be motivated to help young people be creative, play musical instruments, sing, do drama and develop their facilitation skills so that they can help others in their worship.

The list of possible foundational motivations is a very long one. It is to be hoped that our motivations are pure but we perhaps need to recognize that sometimes they might not be. People do things for all sorts of reasons: power; to please people; to massage egos; to feel valued and/or to avoid conflict. Some people simply copy others, without considering what God might be saying or doing.

For Reflection

Spend some time reflecting upon your motivations and see if you can concisely narrow these down to a phrase, sentence or a couple of clear points.

Case Study

Frontier Youth Trust (FYT), the organization I work for, is motivated by the Christian faith and specifically by the call to develop and build *shalom*, and to see justice, equality and community in the lives of 'at risk' young people. FYT employs people who might not share our faith beliefs, but we do ask that they aspire to recognize our motivations and values, and work towards ensuring they manifest these throughout the work of the organization.

What is the Big Idea, Belief or Theory?

6

This is going to sound a bit judgmental, but bear with me. I have met some Christian youth workers who have lots of passion and enthusiasm, a zeal for their faith, but not much else. They are up for doing anything and get very excited by certain approaches and personalities. There is nothing wrong with these characteristics *per se*, but too often such workers lack depth and a clear grounding for their ministry. I would like to see passion and enthusiasm as vehicles outworking the substance and solidity of our characters, thereby enabling us to build work that will be about solid food, not milk (1 Cor 3.2), stand the test of trials and be durable (1 Pet 1.6–7), and be respected by those around us (Acts 6.3).

For me, this is a process that takes time and demands seasons of reflection, revelation, moulding and contemplation as God outworks his purposes—in and through us. I earnestly believe God puts something in each of us that is unique: something that makes us tick; something that makes us feel fully human and something that often does not feel like work when we are involved in it. It might be a specific area of ministry practised in a particular way, a belief in a

> **God puts something in each of us that makes us feel fully human**

key principle that shapes who we are and what we do, or a concept, theory or rationale that gets us out of bed in the morning and drives us on. This idea is represented by the ground floor of the building in my model. I have called this floor the *grounding* upon which we build our work.

I would suggest that Mark Yaconelli's youth ministry is grounded upon the idea of contemplation; Mike Pilavachi's focus is worship; John Ellis in Grimsby, *shalom*; Ruth Valerio, environmental issues; Gemma Dunning, sexuality equality; Dave Andrews, community; Richard Passmore, innovative ways of undertaking mission. We might not have a profile like these people, but this is not the issue. The issue is discovering what it is that God has for us in our work with young people and then living it out. I have met people who have run the youth club tuck shop for decades—this is their big idea; serving others is what their work is grounded upon.

You might not be well-known or influential, but the question is the same whatever our status: what is the big grounding idea for your youth work and ministry, that concept that becomes your master/mistress, not in a bad way, but in a God-way? The Bible uses the word *doulos* to describe someone who gives themself up wholly to another's will, one who gives up their freedom in order to become a slave. Obviously, it is God's will that we give ourselves up to Jesus, whom we seek to serve, but once we have done this I observe that God often gives people a focus, a belief in something very specific or a theoretical imperative they have to outwork. We submit to the master and the master releases us to serve in a specific way.

For Reflection

Simon Frost and Mike Seal say that we should 'take a more philosophical approach' to our work as this will help us 'to be more considered in [our] thinking; helping [us] to argue clearly and precisely about the importance of youth work and the way [we] work with young people.' I believe they are correct in thinking this. In what ways can we take a more philosophical approach? What do we need to consider further? What is it we are arguing our youth work is about? Why is this important?[4]

For me, my big idea is to see young people through a lens of unconditional positive regard. I used to tend to see young people as problems to be solved, people to be changed, who lived lives that could be improved. Now, I see young people more as part of God's wonderful created humanity, full of potential, prospective possibilities and in a much more positive light. This change has impacted my practice and increased my theological understanding to be more in line, I believe, with how God views people.

Case Study

I am currently coaching a couple of volunteer workers who are developing a fresh expression youth-flavoured church on a housing estate in a disadvantaged area of the country. They are very clear about what their big grounding idea is: they want to reach out to the lost generation of young people who live on the estate. Despite having few resources, only a small team of volunteers and lots of young people with challenging behaviour to contend with, they show amazing stickability in their quest to bring good news to a generation that has never heard it.

What Are the Values?

We all live according to a set of values. Some people can easily identify what their own values are, whilst others might struggle to articulate them. Nonetheless, they are present irrespective of whether or not we can vocalize them. These values shape our lives, influence how we perceive God and impact how we work with young people.

For example, if we believe in being creative and see God as creative, we will probably undertake creative work. If we think God is compassionate, kind, caring and loving then it is likely our work will embody these characteristics—in contrast to how our work might look if we think God is a vindictive and harsh judge. If the principle of justice is an important value to us, and we see God as just, it is likely we will embrace that and challenge oppression in the work we do. Our beliefs, values and philosophy shape the work we do.

It is the outworking of our philosophy (*ie* our attitude that acts as a guiding principle for our behaviour) that touches other people; it releases something in us and in others as we engage with them. It is our way of thinking and being, and how we express ourselves because of this, that is important. I observe that without an understood philosophical value base shaping the work we do, it is more difficult to touch people's lives in a positive way.

Without a philosophical value base shaping the work, it is difficult to touch people's lives

There are clearly some common Christian values that specifically shape our work (generosity, truthfulness, forgiveness, love of our neighbours, for example) but there are other more contextual values too. Many of these values do not fit into simple 'right' or 'wrong' boxes. For example, some youth workers believe in small, local projects, whilst others aspire to big, expansive work. Some want to go out and take good news to young people where they are; others believe in gathering young people into an event, church meeting or small group. Strong, directive and single-minded approaches to leadership and decision-making are very important to some people, whilst for others participative, collaborative and multi-voiced approaches take precedent. I like to be open about my feelings, health, vulnerabilities and opinions, but I know other workers are more guarded and private about what they communicate to those they work with and for. We should recognize that not all values are universal and that people have different values that shape their work in unique ways. What is important is that we develop an awareness of what we value, so that we understand how our work is shaped, and how this influences young people.

This shaping and philosophical value base is represented by the first floor in my building model.

Case Study

The research informing this booklet involved undertaking detailed case studies about the values of four Christian-motivated youth work projects. I discovered that these projects had several values in common. They worked in ways that were mutually beneficial for everybody involved—adults, young people and the community. Those involved in the work wanted to see young people thrive, flourish and reach their full potential, irrespective of whether they came to faith or not; the work undertaken was modelling alternative ways of being and living; it had a long-term approach; showed solidarity with the poor and marginalized; and sought to tell positive stories about young people.

How Do You Intend to Go About Your Work?

When talking about developing a model for Christian youth work and faithfully following God, I believe we need to draw on multiple influences in order to establish authenticity for our being and doing. We need to draw on biblical understanding, tradition, history, our personal experience, the experience of others, the needs of those we seek to serve and the influence of contemporary culture in order to determine how we do what we do.

In my model, I call this our 'intentions', and it forms the second floor of my building. What is it we seek to do on a day-to-day basis and what is the method and practice we plan to use in order to facilitate this? What is the practical nature of the work, ministry and education we undertake in order to help young people learn, grow and develop? Educationalists call this our 'pedagogy': the process of understanding and supporting learning.

What is it we seek to do on a day–to–day basis?

We might have an overarching pedagogy that is reflective, creative, critical, nurturing and empowering; or perhaps it is directive, instructive or working to a fixed programme, course, or seasonal pattern of work. My concern is that we take time to think about and put in place a clear set of intentions that will support achieving our *telos*.

In Prov 22.6 we read that we should 'Start children off on the way they should go, and even when they are old they will not turn from it.' Many have used this proverb to justify a strict, disciplined approach to child-rearing. However, I do not believe this is what the original Hebrew language conveys. The sentiment of the words used is more about supporting a young person's future calling, character and natural aptitudes—the things they are made for and predisposed to be and do. In other words, if we can discover what it is a young person is good at, skilled in and passionate about at an early age, we can put in place intentions to support, nurture and develop this so that when they are older they will fulfil their calling. Our job as workers is to support this and my model seeks to embed this as a specific process at both an individual and a collective level.

Case Study

Our intentions need to reflect the shape and philosophical values we have, the grounding we have identified and the motivations positioning our work. If they do not, then we end up with a mismatch between what we say we are about and what we actually do. I worked closely with a church that was trying to develop a strategy for the next season of their work with young people. During the course of my work it became very clear that the content and method of their youth work did not reflect what they said they missionally wanted to do. They said they wanted to reach out and be part of the community, yet everything they did revolved around the church building; the young people in the community were never engaged or touched by anything they did.

What is it You Want to Transform?

God is in the business of transformation—transforming young people and transforming us as we work with them. In secular youth work, many people talk about the transformation that takes place in the lives of young people as 'outcomes.' In simple terms, outcomes are the differences we are realizing in the lives of young people as we work with them. We are encouraged by policymakers to measure these outcomes to prove our value and worth to society as youth workers. This is more than monitoring and evaluating our work, but rather about determining the impact it actually has. This impact and transformation is represented by the third floor of the building in my model.

I am not totally convinced such an approach is particularly godly and I have become a little sceptical and cynical about outcomes-orientated work. We can end up simply engaged in a tick-box culture that is not always honest and all too often tends to do things *to* young people rather than *with* them. As mentioned, such approaches presume young people are lacking in some way and that we have to put this right. I prefer to see young people as human beings full of potential that God wants relationship with in order to bring about transformation, rather than objects we use to justify our own work.

Notwithstanding this, transformation and impact are goals in my model. The type of transformation my model perceives might take decades to become evident. Helping young people fulfil their aspirations, embody hope, become fully thriving and be the people God designed them to be is a lifelong process, not a quick fix. Furthermore, such things are difficult to quantify and measure and we should—if we can—measure successes at each floor of our metaphorical building, not just the end-result extent to which we realize our *telos*. If we can fully measure such transformation, great, but if we cannot, then we need to be internally content that we have built the kingdom in some way. Even the government has acknowledged that 'We know good youth work when we see it' and sometimes this is the best assessment of our work that can be made.[5] Perhaps our responsibility is to simply follow the instructions of the writer in Ecclesiastes and liberally and generously 'Cast your bread on the waters: for you shall find it after many days' (Eccl 11.1). We care for the young people,

Transformation might take decades to become evident

sow seeds as prompted by God and leave him to fulfil the transformation, believing firmly that this will occur.

Case Study

The people who work on the Blend Youth Project in Derbyshire are very clear about what it is they are trying to do. They run a locally rooted, passionate project that is very committed to the young people they work with and the communities they work in. Blend has a strong focus on meeting the needs of local young people, making a difference and realizing transformation as they:

- raise the aspirations of young people;
- develop the self-confidence and self-esteem of young people;
- help young people gain new and practical social skills;
- help young people gain new work-related skills;
- increase opportunities for young people to try new activities;
- empower young people to make better lifestyle choices;
- increase opportunities for young people to achieve accreditations;
- enable young people to access more information, advice and guidance.

There is Always a 'But...' 10

We can have the best youth work and youth work model in the world, but sometimes God just shows up in the most unexpected ways and everything changes. In such circumstances, I will be the first to admit a model might be superseded by the almighty. God is gracious, surprises take place and serendipity is good. We should expect the unexpected when working with God. However, I do not think this entirely negates the need for models to help us organize and deliver the work we do. I also believe that it is not the case that we should have a model instead of God or one that fills a gap until God's spirit moves. The two dynamics are not opposite ends of a spectrum, but approaches that should work hand in hand.

For me, God should be our motivation, inspire our grounding, shape our values, determine our intentions and help us realize our *telos*, which should prevail in our planning and strategizing. These characteristics need to be soaked in prayer and result as a consequence of a journey with God and a reflective practice lifestyle. Furthermore, we can extend the building image / metaphor and perceive not separate isolated floors, but floors interconnected by lots of staircases, mezzanines, balconies and open-plan areas, all representing a way that enables work to flow and come together as the Spirit of God moves, becomes apparent and takes us to new places. It is perhaps this type of image that most fully reflects the complexity and kaleidoscope of possibilities present when God is involved.

We might be in full flow with God and all is well; revival might be in our midst, hurts healed, the sick cured, and the dead being raised. Salaries might be in plentiful supply, volunteers abundant, and people queuing up to be involved. If this is not happening, then maybe we need something that will help support us in what we are called to be and do, something that will help us do it and something that will help us know when we have done it. This is not putting in place mechanisms to give us a helping hand when God is not doing what we think should happen, but more establishing a process and method that maximizes opportunities for God to impact us, enabling us to join with God in his movings.

Conclusion

The model I have set out in this booklet is not meant to be something that restricts or restrains work with young people. I do not suggest it to add to our burdens, but more to provide some reference points for our work from which it can flow and emerge. Furthermore, my model does not intend to put God in a tight little box—or building—but it endeavours, instead, to offer some ideas, structures and processes out of which work can develop.

As a reminder of the model, the following image brings together the key elements of what has been talked about in this booklet:

You may wish to simplify my model or you may desire to build some extra floors to make it more comprehensive. You might think it best to have just one or two simple elements in each floor or you could go for an all-singing and dancing mega construction that covers each possibility and every eventuality. The detail of what happens is very much in your hands. What is hoped is that you give the model a go. See if it works for you and the young people you seek to serve. I would love to know how it works for you and what develops as a result.

You are free, of course, to use another model, a different approach or an alternative strategy. My appeal, however, is that you at least use something. Do not just leave it to chance; do not presume God will just show up and everything will go to plan (he may of course and it might all work out just fine), but instead put things in place to give your vision every chance of succeeding. Establish some stepping stones to get you from where you are now to where you want to be. I think those whom we work for—both young people and adults—deserve at least that.

Notes

1   N Pimlott, *How to Develop a Youth Work Project: Learning from Noah* (Grove Youth booklet Y6).

2   J Pimlott and N Pimlott, *Responding to Challenging Behaviour* (Grove Youth booklet Y1).

3   'Shalom is that encompassing ordering principle and intention, comprising a sense of peace, well-being, welfare, goodness, tranquillity, wholeness, prosperity, justice and security—concepts at the heart of God's purposes. A conceptualization where nothing is broken, nothing is missing and everything is as it was intended to be.' N Pimlott, *Embracing the Passion: Christian Youth Work and Politics* (London: SCM Press, 2015) p 20.

4   S Frost and M Seal, 'Philosophy and Youth Work' in N Stanton (ed), *Innovation in Youth Work: Thinking in Practice* (London: YMCA George William College, 2015) pp 18–21. http://www.ymca.ac.uk/file.php?fileid=352 p 19.

5   House of Commons Education Committee, 'Services for Young People: Third Report of Session 2010–12,' Volume 1, HC 755-1 (London: The Stationery Office Ltd, 2011) p 75.